Every Step Leaves a Footprint

A Journey of Awareness, Growth, and Intentional Living

Shyamankar Singhari

Every Step Leaves a Footprint

Published by WKRISHIND
wkrishind.in

Author: Shyamankar Singhari
Publisher: WKRISHIND

First Edition, 2025

ISBN: 978-81-981954-7-0

Preface

Life is a journey, and every step we take leaves a mark—a footprint that tells the story of who we are, what we value, and how we impact the world. This book is an invitation to walk with awareness, to recognize the significance of each choice, and to shape a path that reflects your deepest intentions.

Every Step Leaves a Footprint was born from a simple yet profound realization: no action is too small to matter. From the quiet thoughts we nurture to the bold decisions we make, every moment contributes to the trail we leave behind. Through stories, reflections, and practical exercises, this book offers a guide to living mindfully, learning from the past, and creating a legacy of purpose and connection.

As you read, I encourage you to pause, reflect, and consider your own journey. What footprints have you left behind? Which ones do you wish to transform, and what kind do you hope to leave moving forward? This book is not about perfection but about presence—about walking through life with intention and grace, knowing that every step shapes the path ahead.

May these pages inspire you to walk consciously, to embrace both the beauty and the challenges of your journey, and to leave footprints that resonate with meaning for yourself and others.

Author's Note

Writing *Every Step Leaves a Footprint* has been a deeply personal journey. The ideas in this book stem from my own experiences—of triumphs, mistakes, fears, and moments of courage that have shaped who I am. I've walked paths I'm proud of and others I've had to retrace with humility. Through it all, I've learned that every step, no matter how small or imperfect, carries a lesson and an opportunity for growth.

This book is not a prescription but a companion. It's designed to meet you wherever you are on your journey, offering tools to reflect, learn, and act with intention. The exercises and reflections included are ones I've used myself, and I hope they serve as gentle guides for you to explore your own footprints. My wish is that these pages help you see the beauty in your journey, embrace the power of your choices, and find joy in creating a path that feels true to you.

Thank you for joining me on this journey. May you find clarity, courage, and inspiration in the steps you take.

– Shyamankar Singhari

Dedication

To those who walk with courage, reflect with honesty, and live with intention—may your footprints light the way for others.

Content

Part 1 — Awareness of Every Step

Chapter 1:

The Power of Small Steps

Life is not always defined by the giant leaps we take, but by the small steps we take every day. Each choice, each action, even the thoughts we nurture quietly, leaves an imprint—not only on ourselves but on the world around us. Like footprints in sand, some are immediately visible, while others are subtle, fading only to reveal their shape later. Yet each one matters.

We often underestimate the ripple of a single moment. Smiling at a stranger, sending a word of encouragement, choosing patience over frustration—these are small steps that quietly shape the course of our journey. Sometimes, we only realize their significance when we look back and see the pattern of our path, the collection of footprints that led us to where we are.

Small steps also include the steps we take inward. Every thought we cultivate, every fear we challenge, every lesson we embrace, becomes a footprint in our mind and soul. Even setbacks are footprints—sometimes messy, sometimes painful—but essential markers that guide our next steps with wisdom.

The beauty of small steps is that they are accessible to everyone. No one needs permission to choose kindness, courage, or reflection. Every step matters because the cumulative effect of these choices creates a life lived with intention rather than by accident.

Take a moment now. Think of one small step you can take today that aligns with the life you want to create. It could be speaking your truth, forgiving a past hurt, or simply pausing to breathe and appreciate this moment. That single step may seem insignificant—but it will leave a footprint. And footprints, no matter how small, always tell a story.

Chapter 2:

Recognizing Your Footprints

We rarely notice the footprints we leave behind. Often, life moves so quickly that we don't pause to see how our actions, words, and choices ripple outward. Yet recognition is the first step toward understanding our journey and shaping the steps to come.

Footprints are more than physical marks—they are the evidence of our presence, the echoes of our intentions. When we speak, act, or even think with awareness, we create patterns that influence ourselves and others. Sometimes, footprints appear in unexpected places: a kind word that lifts someone's spirit, a decision to pursue a dream, or even the quiet courage to face our own fears.

Recognizing your footprints also requires reflection. Ask yourself: What impact have my actions left behind? Which moments reflect my true values? Which ones do I wish had been different? By observing these marks, we begin to understand the story we are writing with our lives.

Not all footprints are perfect. Some are messy or faint; some lead to places we didn't intend. And that is part of the journey. Mistakes, failures, and regrets are footprints too—they are reminders of our growth, markers of lessons learned, and invitations to take better steps moving forward.

When you start noticing your footprints, you become more mindful of the steps you take today. Each moment becomes an opportunity to leave a mark that reflects who you truly want to be. It is not about perfection—it is about presence, awareness, and intention.

Pause for a moment. Reflect on the footprints you've left recently: the choices that align with your values, the actions that have uplifted others, the decisions you may wish to navigate differently. By seeing them clearly, you can decide which footprints to continue leaving and which to transform.

Every step you take matters. And when you recognize the path you've already created, you gain the power to shape the journey ahead with purpose and grace.

Chapter 3:
Mindful Walking

Walking through life often feels automatic. We move from one task to another, react to situations, and sometimes forget to notice the impressions we leave behind. **Mindful walking** is about bringing awareness to each step, each choice, and each moment.

Seeing Your Steps Clearly

When you walk mindfully, you notice the details of your surroundings and the impact of your actions. Every decision, no matter how small, shapes your path and leaves a mark—on yourself and on others. Even simple gestures like a kind word, a smile, or a thoughtful action create footprints that can last longer than you realize.

Practicing Awareness

Mindfulness in action begins with paying attention:

- Observe your feelings before making choices.
- Notice your thoughts and how they influence your behavior.

- Reflect on past actions and recognize the patterns they create.

Small Exercises

1. **Daily Step Reflection**: At the end of each day, write down three actions or decisions you made and consider the footprints they left. Were they positive, neutral, or could they be improved?

2. **Walking Meditation**: Take a slow, deliberate walk, focusing on each step. Feel the ground under your feet, notice your breathing, and observe your thoughts without judgment.

3. **Pause Before Action**: Before responding to situations or people, pause for a moment. Ask yourself: "What kind of footprint will this leave?"

Mindful Walking in Life

Life is a series of steps, both literal and figurative. When you walk mindfully, you start to see the chain of cause and effect—how your choices ripple outward. It becomes easier to choose actions that align with your values and to correct patterns that leave footprints you don't want.

Reflection

Consider the paths you've already walked. What footprints are most visible? Which steps have left marks you are proud of, and which might need gentle correction? Mindful walking allows you to step forward consciously, ensuring that the footprints you leave reflect your best self.

Part 2 — Lessons from the Journey

Chapter 4:

The Footprints of Mistakes

Mistakes are inevitable. Every person leaves imperfect footprints along their journey. Some are small, barely noticeable; others feel heavy, like deep impressions in soft sand. Yet, each mistake carries a lesson—an opportunity to grow, heal, and choose differently.

Understanding the Marks

Mistakes leave footprints that may affect:

- **Yourself**: self-doubt, regret, or insight gained.
- **Others**: misunderstandings, hurt, or unexpected growth in relationships.
- **Your Path**: detours, challenges, or new perspectives on life.

Instead of fearing mistakes, it is vital to recognize them as part of the journey. The footprints they leave are not permanent scars—they are lessons engraved in your story.

Learning Without Regret

Regret can trap us in the past, turning footprints into ruts that prevent forward motion. Learning from mistakes requires reflection:

- Identify what went wrong.
- Accept responsibility without self-condemnation.
- Ask yourself: "What can I do differently next time?"

This mindset transforms footprints of mistakes into stepping stones toward growth.

Small Exercises

1. **Mistake Mapping**: Write down a recent mistake. Trace its effects on yourself and others, then note what you learned.

2. **Lesson Journal**: Keep a section in your journal titled "Footprints of Learning." Each mistake becomes a recorded lesson rather than a mark of failure.

3. **Self-Compassion Pause**: When recalling a mistake, place your hand on your heart, take three deep breaths, and say: "I am learning, and I forgive myself."

Turning Footprints Into Wisdom

Every misstep carries wisdom. By reflecting and adjusting, your footprints shift from negative impressions to meaningful lessons. Over time, the paths you walk become richer, informed by the awareness of past choices and the courage to walk anew.

Reflection

Look at your journey so far. Which mistakes have left the deepest footprints? Which have taught you the most about yourself? Accept these marks as evidence of growth, not failure. The footprints of mistakes, when observed consciously, become guiding steps toward a more mindful, intentional life.

Chapter 5:
Footprints of Kindness

Every action we take leaves a mark, but few marks are as profound as those of kindness. Acts of love, generosity, and compassion create ripples that extend far beyond the immediate moment. Unlike mistakes, which often feel heavy, the footprints of kindness uplift, inspire, and transform both giver and receiver.

The Power of Small Acts

Kindness doesn't have to be grand to leave a lasting impression. Simple gestures—smiling at a stranger, listening attentively, offering help—can ripple outward in unexpected ways. Each small step of care contributes to a path lined with positivity and connection.

- **Personal Impact**: Kindness nurtures your own sense of purpose and joy.

- **Impact on Others**: Even a brief act of consideration can shift someone's day, mindset, or choices.

- **Wider Influence**: One kind act can inspire others to act with generosity, creating a chain of meaningful footprints.

Cultivating a Habit of Kindness

Kindness becomes transformative when practiced intentionally. It's about noticing moments where your actions can matter. Questions to guide you:

- Can I help without expecting anything in return?
- Am I offering encouragement or understanding when it's needed?
- How can I leave someone's day a little brighter than I found it?

Small, consistent acts build a trail of light along your journey.

Exercises to Leave Kind Footprints

1. **Daily Kindness Challenge**: Each day, intentionally perform one act of kindness. Reflect in your journal how it made you feel and what impact you noticed.

2. **Kindness Mapping**: Track where your kindness has reached. Note both the obvious and subtle effects.

3. **Gratitude Reflection**: When someone shows you kindness, acknowledge it. Record how it affected you—this

strengthens awareness of reciprocal footprints.

Reflection

Think of the last time someone's kindness impacted you deeply. How did it shape your thoughts or actions afterward? Now, consider your own actions—what kind footprints are you leaving behind? The path of life becomes richer and more connected when marked by intentional compassion.

Kindness leaves footprints not just on the world but in your heart, shaping the journey for both yourself and those around you.

Chapter 6:
Footprints of Fear

Fear is a powerful force. It influences choices, shapes habits, and can leave deep imprints on our journey. Unlike kindness, which uplifts, or courage, which propels us forward, fear often leaves footprints that weigh us down, limit possibilities, and create invisible barriers. Yet, understanding these footprints is the first step to transforming them.

Recognizing the Marks of Fear

Fear shows up in many forms: hesitation, self-doubt, avoidance, or overthinking. Every time we let fear dictate our actions—or inactions—we leave a trail that can shape our present and future. Common footprints of fear include:

- **Missed Opportunities**: Choosing safety over growth, leaving dreams unpursued.
- **Strained Relationships**: Avoiding vulnerability or honesty out of fear of rejection.
- **Internal Conflict**: Doubts and "what-ifs" that replay in the mind, creating stress or anxiety.

Understanding the Source

Fear is not inherently bad—it's a survival mechanism designed to protect us. However, when it dominates our decisions, it leaves heavy footprints that hold us back. Reflection questions:

- What patterns in my life are shaped by fear?
- Which fears are rational, and which are holding me unnecessarily?
- How have my past fears influenced my present choices?

Transforming Fear into Awareness

The key is not to eliminate fear, but to acknowledge it and learn from it. Every footprint of fear can become a stepping stone for growth. Techniques to transform fear:

1. **Mindful Observation**: Notice when fear influences a decision. Write down what you feel and why.
2. **Small Steps Toward Courage**: Break down fearful actions into manageable steps. Each small success weakens fear's grip.

3. **Reframing Fear**: View fear as a signal, not a stop sign. Ask, "What can this fear teach me?"

Exercises to Heal Fearful Footprints

- **Fear Journal**: Record moments when fear influenced your choices. Reflect on alternative actions that courage could have enabled.

- **Visualization**: Imagine taking the step you fear most. Visualize success and the relief that comes from moving forward.

- **Affirmations of Strength**: Create a list of phrases to remind yourself that fear is temporary and you are capable.

Reflection

Look at your recent decisions—how many were guided by fear? Which footprints do you want to transform into marks of courage and growth? Fear is part of every journey, but with awareness, it can guide rather than limit you.

Fear leaves footprints—but they do not have to define the path. Every step taken with conscious courage transforms those marks into lessons and growth.

Chapter 7:

Footprints of Courage

Courage is not the absence of fear—it is the decision to move forward despite it. While fear leaves heavy, limiting footprints, courage creates marks of strength, resilience, and possibility. Every act of bravery, no matter how small, leaves an imprint that shapes your character and inspires those around you.

Understanding Courage

Courage often appears quietly in daily life. It is the choice to speak up, to try again after failure, or to embrace vulnerability. Unlike dramatic heroic acts, the footprints of courage are subtle yet enduring. Examples include:

- **Facing Difficult Conversations**: Expressing truth even when it's uncomfortable.
- **Pursuing Personal Goals**: Taking steps toward a dream despite doubt or risk.
- **Overcoming Setbacks**: Choosing resilience over resignation when life challenges you.

The Connection Between Fear and Courage

Courage and fear are intertwined. Without fear, courage would have no context. Recognizing fear allows you to consciously choose courage. Reflection questions:

- When has fear held me back?
- How did I act courageously despite fear?
- Which areas of my life could benefit from a courageous step today?

Cultivating Courage

Courage can be strengthened like a muscle. Consistent practice builds confidence and reduces the power of fear. Strategies to cultivate courage:

1. **Small Daily Risks**: Take manageable actions outside your comfort zone. Even small victories reinforce your ability to act courageously.
2. **Visualize Success**: Picture yourself facing challenges with confidence and clarity.
3. **Celebrate Courageous Acts**: Recognize every moment of bravery, no matter how small—it fuels your self-belief.

Exercises to Leave Courageous Footprints

- **Courage List**: Write down actions you've taken recently that required bravery. Reflect on how each has shaped you.

- **Fear-to-Courage Mapping**: Identify a fear, then list one courageous action you can take to overcome it.

- **Daily Courage Practice**: Commit to one act of courage each day, whether it's emotional, social, or practical.

Reflection

Look at your life and notice where courage has left its footprints. Each step taken in bravery builds momentum, reshapes your path, and inspires growth. Courage transforms hesitation into movement, fear into possibility, and challenges into lessons.

Every courageous step leaves a lasting mark—not just on your journey, but on the lives of those you encounter.

Part 3 — Navigating the Path

Chapter 8:
Choosing Your Path Wisely

Life is a series of choices, and each step we take shapes the journey ahead. Some paths lead to growth, joy, and fulfillment, while others bring stagnation, regret, or unnecessary struggle. Choosing wisely requires awareness, reflection, and intentionality.

The Power of Choice

Every decision, big or small, leaves a footprint. Even seemingly insignificant actions influence your mindset, relationships, and future opportunities. By consciously evaluating your choices, you ensure that your footprints align with your values and long-term goals.

Ask yourself:

- Does this choice reflect who I truly am?
- Will this path help me grow or hold me back?
- Am I acting from clarity or impulse?

Recognizing Patterns

Often, we repeat paths that feel familiar, even if they are not beneficial. Recognizing these patterns allows you to make new, more conscious choices.

- **Past Footprints**: Reflect on previous decisions. Which led to growth? Which caused setbacks?

- **Current Alignment**: Are your present actions consistent with your values and aspirations?

- **Future Vision**: Imagine where your current path may lead in 1, 5, or 10 years.

Tools for Wise Decision-Making

1. **Pause and Reflect**: Before acting, take a moment to assess your options and their potential impact.

2. **Seek Guidance**: Mentors, trusted friends, or reflective practices like journaling can illuminate choices you may not see clearly.

3. **Listen to Intuition**: Your inner voice often knows the right direction—learn to trust it.

4. **Consider Long-Term Consequences**: Short-term gains may come at the cost of meaningful footprints.

Exercises to Choose Wisely

- **Path Mapping**: Write down current decisions or dilemmas, outlining potential outcomes for each option.
- **Value Alignment Check**: List your top five values and evaluate whether your choices honor them.
- **Footprint Forecast**: Imagine the legacy your decisions may leave on yourself and others.

Reflection

Choosing your path wisely is not about perfection; it's about conscious action. Even if mistakes occur, awareness helps you redirect with intention. Each thoughtful step ensures that your journey reflects your authentic self, leaving meaningful footprints that guide your future and inspire others.

Remember: the steps you take today define the trails you leave behind. Choose with awareness, act with purpose, and walk confidently toward the life you wish to create.

Chapter 9:

Rewriting Old Trails

Our past is like a trail through the forest—some paths are bright and clear, while others are overgrown with mistakes, regrets, or unresolved emotions. But no trail is permanent. Just as nature reshapes paths over time, we have the power to rewrite the trails of our past and transform old footprints into lessons for growth.

Understanding Old Footprints

Old trails often carry patterns of thought, behavior, and emotion that no longer serve us. They might appear as:

- **Regret** over past decisions
- **Guilt** about how we treated ourselves or others
- **Fear** of repeating mistakes

Recognizing these patterns is the first step in rewriting them. Awareness allows you to separate the lessons from the pain, giving you control over the story your past tells.

Rewriting the Narrative

1. **Acceptance**: Begin by accepting what has happened without judgment. Accepting the past doesn't mean condoning mistakes—it means freeing yourself from the emotional weight that keeps you stuck.

2. **Reflection**: Examine the choices and actions that led to old footprints. What triggered them? What did you learn? How have they shaped your present?

3. **Reframing**: Turn regrets into insights. Instead of thinking, "I failed," try, "I learned what doesn't work, and now I can choose differently."

4. **Intentional Action**: Actively create new footprints that align with your values and aspirations. Replace patterns of self-doubt with actions of self-respect and courage.

Healing Old Wounds

Old trails often carry emotional residue. Writing, therapy, or guided reflection can help process lingering feelings. By addressing the past with compassion and clarity, you prevent it from controlling your present steps.

Exercises to Rewrite Old Trails

- **Trail Journaling**: Write down a memory or pattern you want to change. Reflect on what you learned and how you can act differently moving forward.

- **Footprint Swap**: Identify one negative behavior or thought pattern. Replace it with a positive, intentional action and repeat until it becomes natural.

- **Visualization**: Close your eyes and imagine walking an old trail. Picture removing obstacles, planting new signs, and walking confidently toward a brighter path.

Reflection

Rewriting old trails is a courageous act. It doesn't erase the past, but it transforms its impact. By acknowledging, reframing, and acting intentionally, you leave new footprints—trails that reflect growth, wisdom, and resilience.

Remember: your past is not a chain; it's a map. With conscious steps, you can navigate it differently, leaving a path that guides your future and inspires others to do the same.

Chapter 10:
Walking With Others

Life is not a solitary journey. Every step we take interacts with the footsteps of others—family, friends, mentors, and even strangers. Recognizing the impact of relationships on our paths allows us to walk more consciously, creating shared footprints of growth, support, and connection.

The Influence of Others

Every person we encounter leaves a mark on our trail:

- **Supportive Guides**: Those who encourage, teach, or inspire us.
- **Challenging Companions**: People whose actions test our patience, boundaries, or resilience.
- **Silent Witnesses**: Individuals who may not directly influence us but whose presence reminds us of who we are and what we value.

Being aware of these influences helps us choose our company wisely and understand how others shape our journey.

Walking Together Intentionally

1. **Mutual Respect**: Walking with someone means honoring each other's path, not controlling or overshadowing it.

2. **Shared Goals**: Aligning with people who share your values or aspirations can amplify growth and motivation.

3. **Support and Accountability**: Trusted companions can offer guidance, encouragement, and honest feedback when the trail gets rough.

4. **Celebrating Differences**: Not every step will match perfectly; diversity in perspectives enriches your journey and strengthens resilience.

Navigating Conflicts

Not all footprints are positive. Conflicts, misunderstandings, or betrayals can leave deep impressions. Instead of avoiding or resenting these moments:

- **Learn the Lesson**: Examine what the situation reveals about yourself, your triggers, and your values.

- **Set Boundaries**: Protect your path from repeated harm while remaining compassionate.

- **Choose Forgiveness**: Forgiveness is for your own freedom, not necessarily for the other person.

Exercises for Walking With Others

- **Mapping Connections**: Draw a map of key relationships and identify how each influences your journey. Reflect on who uplifts you, who challenges you, and who requires healthy distance.

- **Shared Footprints Exercise**: Choose someone whose path intersects with yours. Write down how you positively impact each other's journeys and how you can support growth mutually.

- **Boundary Reflection**: Identify areas where you need to protect your path. Practice expressing your needs clearly and kindly.

Reflection

Walking with others transforms a solitary trail into a rich tapestry of shared experiences. By choosing companions intentionally, respecting differences, and learning from conflicts, your journey becomes more meaningful and your footprints more impactful.

Remember: while your path is uniquely yours, the footprints of those you walk with shape the direction, texture, and depth of your life's journey.

Part 4 — Leaving a Lasting Legacy

Chapter 11:
Footprints for the Future

Every step you take today leaves a trace that stretches into tomorrow. Your actions, words, and choices shape not only your own path but also the lives of those who follow or cross your trail. Understanding the long-term impact of your footprints encourages intentional living and inspires a legacy that resonates beyond your lifetime.

The Power of Intention

Intentionality transforms ordinary steps into meaningful marks. Before acting or speaking, pause to ask yourself:

- Will this choice contribute positively to my growth and the growth of others?
- Does this align with the values I want to leave behind?
- How might this decision be remembered in the future?

Small, conscious decisions compounded over time create profound effects. Like ripples in water, even minor footprints influence distant shores.

Creating Positive Impact

1. **Lead by Example**: Demonstrate integrity, kindness, and resilience. Others notice footprints of character more than words.

2. **Empower Others**: Share knowledge, encouragement, and support. Guiding someone along their journey multiplies the influence of your footprints.

3. **Cultivate Gratitude and Generosity**: Acts of appreciation and giving leave impressions of warmth and connection that endure.

4. **Document Your Journey**: Journaling lessons, stories, and reflections provides a roadmap for future generations—literally leaving footprints in written form.

Preparing for Unseen Footprints

Not all impacts are immediately visible. Some choices only reveal their influence years later. Trust that conscious actions create unseen but meaningful marks:

- Plant seeds of growth today that may blossom in the future.

- Practice patience and resilience; your steady footsteps inspire others silently.

- Let your values guide decisions even when the outcomes are uncertain.

Exercises for Leaving Lasting Footprints

- **Legacy Reflection**: Write down what you want your footprints to reflect ten, twenty, or fifty years from now. Identify steps you can take today to align with that vision.

- **Impact Map**: Sketch a map of people, places, and communities your actions touch. Note ways to expand positive influence consciously.

- **Future Self Letter**: Write a letter to your future self describing the footprints you hope to leave behind and the values guiding them.

Reflection

The footprints you leave today are the seeds of tomorrow's paths. Living with awareness and purpose ensures that your journey becomes a source of inspiration, guidance, and hope for yourself and others. By acting intentionally, every step you take contributes to a legacy of growth, love, and meaningful connection.

Chapter 12:

Reflecting on the Journey

Reflection is the bridge between experience and wisdom. By looking back at the paths you've walked, you gain clarity about the choices you made, the lessons learned, and the footprints you've left behind. Reflection is not about dwelling on regrets but about understanding, appreciating, and learning from your journey.

Why Reflection Matters

Life moves quickly, and without pause, our footprints can blur into the background. Reflection allows you to:

- Recognize patterns in your decisions and actions.
- Celebrate growth and accomplishments, no matter how small.
- Identify areas where change or improvement is possible.
- Gain perspective on challenges and hardships.

Steps for Meaningful Reflection

1. **Pause and Observe**: Take time to mentally walk through your recent

experiences. Notice what felt significant, challenging, or transformative.

2. **Ask Insightful Questions:**

    - What lessons did this chapter of life teach me?
    - Which footprints am I proud of?
    - Where could I have acted differently, and what would I do now?

3. **Write It Down**: Journaling your reflections transforms fleeting thoughts into tangible insights. Document both triumphs and struggles.

4. **Celebrate Progress**: Recognize the growth that comes from even the smallest steps. Reflection is a way to honor your journey and yourself.

Learning from Both Success and Struggle

Every footprint, whether born of courage or mistake, has something to teach. Success shows what works; struggle teaches resilience and adaptation. By reflecting on both, you create a richer understanding of your life's path.

- **Footprints of Joy**: Remember moments of happiness, connection, and accomplishment. Let them inspire future steps.

- **Footprints of Challenge**: Recognize hardships not as failures but as opportunities for growth and learning.

Exercises for Reflection

- **Journey Timeline**: Draw a timeline of significant events in your life. Mark the "footprints" that left the most lasting impact. Reflect on patterns and lessons.

- **Gratitude Walk**: Walk mindfully and recall moments that shaped your life positively. Acknowledge the people and experiences that influenced your journey.

- **Reflective Letter**: Write a letter to your past self, highlighting the lessons learned and offering encouragement for the steps yet to come.

Reflection as a Compass

The practice of reflection serves as a compass for your next steps. By understanding your past, you can move forward with awareness, intention, and confidence, ensuring that your future footprints are conscious and meaningful.

Chapter 13:
Stepping Forward with Intention

Every step you take has the potential to leave a meaningful footprint. Yet, without conscious thought, we often move through life on autopilot, leaving behind traces we neither choose nor understand. Stepping forward with intention means acting with awareness, purpose, and a clear sense of direction.

What It Means to Move with Intention

Intentional living is about aligning your actions with your values, goals, and the kind of legacy you want to leave. It is a deliberate choice to:

- Live consciously rather than reactively.
- Make decisions that reflect your deepest beliefs and desires.
- Shape the impact you leave on others and yourself.

Principles for Intentional Steps

1. **Clarity of Purpose**: Know what matters most to you. Your values, passions, and priorities will guide your actions.

2. **Mindful Decision-Making**: Pause before acting. Consider the short- and long-term consequences of your choices.

3. **Consistency and Discipline**: Small, intentional actions repeated over time create lasting footprints.

4. **Adaptability and Reflection**: Even intentional steps may lead to unexpected outcomes. Use them as opportunities to learn and adjust.

Practices to Cultivate Intentionality

- **Daily Check-In**: Each morning, set a clear intention for the day. Ask yourself, "What kind of footprints do I want to leave today?"

- **End-of-Day Reflection**: Review your actions and choices. Celebrate intentional steps and identify moments to improve.

- **Visualize the Path**: Imagine the life and impact you want to create. Visualization strengthens focus and commitment.

- **Prioritize Meaningful Actions**: Align your energy with activities that contribute to your personal growth, relationships, and goals.

Overcoming Obstacles

Living intentionally is not always easy. Distractions, habits, fear, and uncertainty can pull you off course. Recognize these obstacles without judgment and gently steer yourself back toward purposeful action. Intentional living is a practice, not a perfection.

The Ripple Effect

Intentional steps don't just shape your own life —they influence those around you. Every conscious action, word, and decision sends ripples through your relationships, community, and environment. By stepping forward with purpose, you create a positive chain reaction of thoughtful footprints.

Exercise for Intentional Living

- **Footprint Map**: Draw or list the actions you want to take in the coming week that align with your values. Reflect on the footprints each step may leave and adjust as needed.

- **Intention Journal**: Write down your intentions daily, review at the end of the day, and note moments where your actions reflected your true self.

Closing Thought

Each day offers countless opportunities to leave footprints that matter. By stepping forward with intention, you ensure that the traces you leave behind reflect your best self, contribute meaningfully to the world, and guide you toward a life of purpose and fulfillment.

Closing Summary: The Journey of Your Footprints

Life is a series of steps—each one leaving its mark on your journey, your relationships, and the world around you. *Every Step Leaves Footprints* is a reminder that nothing is truly insignificant. The choices you make, the actions you take, and even the thoughts you nurture all leave impressions—traces that influence your present and future.

Key Takeaways

1. **Awareness of Every Step**
   - Every action, no matter how small, carries weight. Cultivating mindfulness in daily life helps you recognize the footprints you leave behind.
2. **Learning from the Past**

- Reflect on past mistakes, kindness, fears, and courage. Each experience offers lessons that can guide future decisions and help reshape old patterns.

3. **The Power of Intention**
    - Stepping forward with purpose transforms ordinary actions into meaningful contributions. Intentional living ensures your footprints reflect your values and goals.

4. **Mindful Relationships**
    - Your interactions leave lasting marks on others. By cultivating empathy, kindness, and clear communication, you can positively shape your connections and the world around you.

5. **Healing and Transformation**
    - Negative or unintended footprints are not permanent. Through reflection, self-compassion, and deliberate action, you can transform past patterns into growth and insight.

6. **Creating a Legacy**

    - Consider the long-term impact of your choices. Strive to leave footprints that inspire, support, and uplift others—beyond your immediate surroundings.

7. **Daily Practices for Conscious Living**

    - Journaling, reflection, mindful walking, and visualization are tools to help you maintain awareness, learn from experiences, and align actions with intentions.

Final Thought

Your life is a path marked by countless footprints. Some are bold, some subtle—but all matter. By embracing awareness, learning from the journey, and stepping forward with intention, you can ensure that your footprints tell a story of growth, love, courage, and purpose.

Remember: every step matters. Every choice echoes. Every footprint shapes the journey ahead. Walk consciously, live intentionally, and leave a trail worth following.

9 788198 195470

Printed at Repro India Ltd.